Self-Service IT: Just Plug In v.1

Cartoons & Commentary

By Thomas A. Tinsley
Copyright © 2009 Thomas A. Tinsley
www.SelfServiceIT.com

Tinsley, Thomas A.

Self-Service IT: Just Plug In v.1

Thomas A. Tinsley, - 1st ed.

ISBN: 1449597424   EAN-13: 9781449597429

1. Enterprise Architecture 2. Management
3. Technological Innovation. 4. Diffusion of Innovations.
5. Information Technology. 6. Information Society.
7. Organizational change.

I. Tinsley, Thomas A. II. Title

Library of Congress Control Number: 2009912894

Chief Editor: Janet Tyrrell Tinsley

Cover by: Thomas A. Tinsley and Rodney T. Tinsley

Produced by: **Tinsley Innovations**

Preface

If you are in business, then your Enterprise Architect can be your best friend. Like any best friend, you will receive the devotion and concern of someone that can give you unconditional support.

Your Enterprise Architect is always on the side of the business, your side. There are no better listeners or communicators.

Having a friend that understands the deep dark mysteries of the Corporate IT group is a good friend to have. This is a friend that will go with you to the Board Room. This is a friend that will travel deep into the territory of IT, the territory of the "Lords of the Underworld", and do battle on your behalf.

In this brief text, you will learn how the Enterprise Architect can be your friend and stand by your side during these changing times. This text originally appeared as entries on my blog: www.SelfServiceIT.com. You can follow the blog to find and learn more.

If you want greater detail showing what to expect of an Enterprise Architect, get a copy of the book *Enterprise Architects: Masters of the Unseen City.* You will find that you, too, can see the unseen with the help of your good friend, the Enterprise Architect.

If you do not have an Enterprise Architect as a friend, then get one. Otherwise, you risk being left behind by your competition as they architect with their best friend.

The overall theme is self-service IT. This is a shift of control from Corporate IT back to the corporate lines-of-business. The shift is inevitable. With an Enterprise Architect as a friend, your shift towards independence can move more rapidly.

Table of Contents

Introducing Self-Service IT

Enterprise Architects are Misunderstood

- Thomas A. Tinsley

We are on the road to a major change in the deployment of Information Technology. We have reached a breaking point. Complexity of IT is getting in the way of corporate success. We need new approaches. We need to move up a level in our thinking. We need to see the entire corporate enterprise's application of Information Technology.

Events are taking place every day that are moving us down this road. These are the events where new concepts and approaches are being introduced. It is these events that I have highlighted in this book.

In my first book, *Deadlines and Duct Tape*[1], I offered personal stories of how IT will always try to stay within budgets and schedules. They often can only accomplish this by lowering quality with "quick and dirty" solutions. The case is presented that the constant application of these "duct tape" solutions by IT is actually a Corporate Management problem. Corporate Management is simply rewarding the wrong behavior. Unfortunately, the entire complexity of IT is invisible to Corporate Management. This makes it difficult for them to understand all of the ramifications of the multitude of IT decisions.

In my second book, *Enterprise Architects: Masters of the Unseen City*[2], I unveil the heroes that are bringing the visibility of IT to Corporate Managers. They are the Enterprise Architects.

The profession of Enterprise Architect is not well understood. Many still see Enterprise Architects as

[1] Thomas A. Tinsley, *Deadlines and Duct Tape* (Tampa, FL: Meghan-Kiffer Press, 2008).

[2] Thomas A. Tinsley, *Enterprise Architects: Masters of the Unseen City* (New Port Richey, FL: Tinsley Innovations, 2009).

Solution Architects, Infrastructure Architects, or Communications Architects. In the Enterprise Architecture community there is a consensus that the business comes first and technology is only the means to reach the business goals.

The organization, Center for the Advancement of the Enterprise Architect Profession, (CAEAP), is working to put more definition to this new profession. The CAEAP shows the vision, mission, goals, and core values of the Enterprise Architect profession. Read more about CAEAP at http://www.caeap.org.

The heroes, Enterprise Architects, are the guides that will help corporations down the road by finding new ways to bring visibility to IT. Each step down the road will move us closer to the illuminated city on the hill, the IT City. This is the city where innovation flourishes.

Control Information Technology Yourself

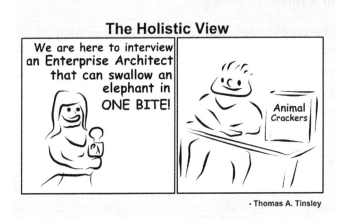

- Thomas A. Tinsley

CITY is an acronym for "Control Information Technology Yourself". It represents a movement of corporate managers that no longer have a fear of computers. It represents the new generation where everyone is connected and sharing. It represents the beginning of an unprecedented explosion in innovation.

Long before computers were available, corporate managers knew exactly how every transaction in their organization worked. They could walk through the paper trail and discover problems, answer questions, and apply improvements. When IBM introduced their first business machines based on punched cards, things did not change much. The corporate manager could still see where the information was being keyed, sorted, collated, and merged.

This visibility held by corporate managers that had existed for thousands of years was completely lost when computers began executing the business process steps. At first, every step was done in a batch process with job names that could be easily translated to actual business processes. In time, the jobs became larger by the addition of enhanced functionality. It was no longer easy to correlate single business functions with job steps. Then, more and more transactions were processed in real-time for a multitude of business functions. What was once so easily seen by corporate managers has now become invisible to them.

The Corporate Information Technology organizations now control the life blood information of the corporation. The computing lights must stay on for an organization to survive. Continuous improvements must provide enhancements for a corporation to stay competitive, within the law, and secure.

The Corporate Information Technology organizations are deemed as necessary by the Corporate Office even though enhancement outcomes are not always what they expect. These concerns arise as corporate managers make major changes in their own spreadsheets in minutes while IT enhancements seem to take an enormous amount of time and money.

With the help of Enterprise Architects, the CITY will soon be in view. Corporate managers will be returned to their position of control where innovation, driven by those in the business, will shape the future of competitiveness.

Enabling the Crowd by Enterprise Architects

Enabling the Crowd

- Thomas A. Tinsley

Once again, IBM is proving that they understand the direction of the use of Information Technology. Last week I attended the IBM webinar: "IBM's Approach to Working Smarter". It opened with a presentation by James Surowiecki, author of *The Wisdom of Crowds*[3]. It then followed with some statistics and an update on

---

3 James Surowiecki, *The Wisdom of Crowds* (New York, NY: Anchor Books, 2005).

IBM products that support the changing business environment.

In a fairly obvious manner, IBM is saying that the centralized control of IT should move to a more open, business environment. In this environment, social networking software can be used to advance the application of technology. In my language, that directly relates to the CITY (Control Information Technology Yourself).

Innovation must move to the business. When only IT provides innovation, the ideas are limited to the professionals in IT. By opening up the involvement of the crowd as described by Surowiecke, not only does the amount of contribution increase, but so does the quality.

In the webinar, IBM backed up their statements with an IBM survey that reported that 98% of CEOs plan to restructure the way their organization works. I believe that this is a very powerful statement. IBM followed with some survey statements from CIOs, but I tend to disregard these statements. I disregard them for the very reason IBM focused on the <u>wisdom of the crowds</u>. The way out, the way to restructure how organizations work, should be based upon the crowd. Why do the very opposite and look only to the IT experts for answers?

One reason that IBM must look to the CIOs for answers is because it requires IT organizations to install, maintain, and utilize the IBM products. Collaboration from IBM is supported with IBM Lotus® and IBM WebSphere®. Business process is supported with IBM BPM Suite and Operations Strategy services. These are highly technical facilities that would be integrated into the complex technical infrastructure that only experts understand.

I believe what is missing in the IBM approach to "work smarter" is the Enterprise Architect. The Enterprise Architect, working within the organization's Strategic Planning function, could expose a visual layer of the organization's current use of IT. This visual layer would then allow each line of business to collaborate and build business processes without the direct involvement of a corporate IT organization.

This visual layer would enhance the visual development of business processes and expand ongoing collaboration. It would accomplish this by providing a common language for dialog and an understanding of the existing IT services. The common language would eliminate the "Tower of Babble" currently surrounding

IT. The understanding of services would come from being able to see all of the current business integration points available within the IT infrastructure.

The Enterprise Architect would act as the facilitator to have a better informed crowd. With the unseen exposed, collaboration would cause unprecedented innovation. Business processes would be applied in more ways than currently considered. In the end, as IBM would say, we would be "working smarter".

Tools for Enterprise Architecture

- Thomas A. Tinsley

Recently, at an Enterprise Architecture conference, the speaker asked several hundred attendees what tools they used. The majority of them raised their hand when he asked about Visio. Everyone laughed. But unfortunately, this is not a joke.

The lack of well-defined tools to support the profession of Enterprise Architect is a strong indicator that the profession has not yet matured. For an industry that is founded on technology, how could we still find ourselves doing artwork? Enterprise Architecture should be based upon highly-disciplined engineering principles.

So where are those principles? Have Zachman, Yourdon, and a host of others been wrong? Is there not an enterprise view above the Unified Modeling Language?

I believe that the principles already exist and they will only get better. The problem is not the principles. It is the attitude of the messenger. It is the attitude of the Enterprise Architects who believe they are solution providers. With this attitude, they believe their purpose is to present to management, in the simplest form possible, a strategy for IT. They like to say they are all about the business. Some even believe that only the future is important and there should be no attention given to fully understanding the current environment.

So what should the attitude be? The attitude that best supports the business is one that recognizes that those that run the business are more than capable of understanding the Enterprise Architecture. They are more than capable of making the big decisions necessary to direct the overall strategy. The Enterprise Architects should be the facilitators in making this happen.

When the Enterprise Architects shed themselves of believing they are the solution providers, we can then begin to see some progress towards principles. We would see commonalities in approaches in all organizations. Managers could move from one organization to another and be able to quickly understand the strategy for IT. Universities would include Enterprise Architecture as part of their business curriculum just as they do Marketing, Finance, etc.

With this attitude change, the principles will become apparent. This will happen when Enterprise Architects realize that the business managers are not customers, but partners. Business managers are the owners that take risks by investing in IT. They take these risks to either reduce costs or increase revenues. Enterprise Architects must provide them with the pertinent information so they can minimize their risk.

With this change in attitude, the principles will rise to the surface. The products will be developed to support the principles. Then, at long last, the Enterprise Architects will have tools for their profession.

Enterprise Architects Make Preparation for the Storm

Cloud computing is a hot topic. There are multitudes of articles and books pouring out to help us all better understand this new wave. We have to dig in so we can uncover the differences between a public cloud, a private cloud, and a hybrid. And then, there are new standards being developed so applications can move to any cloud and all clouds can share messages.

Some see the cloud as just another way to provision hardware, similar in concept to virtualization. Some see the cloud as "Software as a Service". This comes as an expansion on the whole Service-Oriented Architecture approach.

Well, everyone is probably right, but no one actually knows how the cloud computing phenomenon will turn out. But, like most things, we may only need to follow the money. In the end, cloud computing will reduce costs. Hardware costs will go down because there will be greater usage of the cloud equipment. The greater usage means the users will pay less for their amount of consumption. As corporations flock to business services available in the cloud, then there will be greater competition and again the cost will go down.

So, to take a broad look at this shift, let's compare it to other historical shifts. The original business machines from IBM used punched cards to pull information processing out of each line-of-business unit into a centralized function. This was usually placed in Accounting. When this equipment was replaced by large mainframe computers, the processing function moved out of Accounting and became its own organization. This organization took care of all of the hardware and software for the entire business.

Frustration was high for the business users waiting on solutions from the centralized IT, so the situation was ripe for the introduction of the PC. Business users jumped on spreadsheet and word-processing software without hesitation. The IBM PC did exceptionally well, because the business folks believed that they would get access to their IBM mainframe data and processes.

The next big change was the internet. Unfortunately, the dreamers and investors did not fully deliver. But, even though there was a bust, many great services did survive and the internet is now a part of everyone's life.

So what can be said about the cloud? I believe it is more about control than about money. Business users wanted control and that is what drove the purchasing of PCs. PCs were certainly not inexpensive at that time. The internet, by its nature, is about personal access and control. The cloud is heading down this path.

Information Technology groups have had their control of software chipped away over the years with packaged software and outsourced development. Now, due to cloud computing, the data center is about to be outsourced.

My belief is that it will be up to the Enterprise Architects to bring clarity to this transition. It is a transition of control of Information Technology from the Corporate IT departments back to the line-of-business units. This will take us back to the form of business control that existed before the first punched card. This will put control in the hands of those who can provide the greatest level of innovation.

What is an Enterprise Architect?

- Thomas A. Tinsley

The name, Enterprise Architect, does not provide any real sense of meaning. Enterprise Architects profess to be about the business first and technology second. Does this mean they see themselves as architecting the entire business? Are they vying for the role of Corporate President?

What do they want to architect? Do they want to determine all of the technologies used by Information Technology and any other automation in the enterprise?

Do they want to architect all projects? Where does their scope of concern end?

With a name like Enterprise Architect, it is easy to see where it might be interpreted as wanting to take over the business on one end and all technologies on the other.

Generally, interpretation is not a problem, because the role of Enterprise Architect is not recognized by most corporate offices. The name is usually associated with Information Technology, so the assumption is that this role is part of the CIO's responsibility. In some cases this may be appropriate, but in most, it is incorrect to assume that Enterprise Architects belong in IT.

In some rare cases, the CIO is a strategic planner and knows exactly how to charter and support the Enterprise Architects. In these cases, the CIO knows how to accept the governance that comes from the Enterprise Architects to improve short and long-range quality. Unfortunately, in most organizations the CIO is committed to project delivery dates and will give in to short-term gains over sound structural architecture.

Because Enterprise Architecture is often assumed to be part of Corporate IT, the role gets associated with technical functions or project solutions. There is confusion about the difference between an Enterprise

Architect and a host of other names such as Infrastructure Architect, Solutions Architect, Network Architect, etc.

The first step in understanding Enterprise Architects is to know where to place them in an organization. They are top-down and strategic by nature, so they should be placed in the organization where they can bring value through facilitation and communication. They also have an in-depth knowledge of Information Technology processes and facilities that allows them to present simplified views of an otherwise complex environment.

The second step must come from the Enterprise Architects themselves. They must reach a point of being able to clearly describe what their role is about and how it brings value to an organization. The work being done by the Center for the Advancement of the Enterprise Architecture Profession (CAEAP) is a good beginning.

In the end, the name will be less important than the interpretation that others have when they hear the name. Will everyone have positive thoughts like when they hear the name "nurse" or will there be a less than positive response like hearing the name "lawyer".

Enterprise Architecture and E-Discovery

- Thomas A. Tinsley

E-Discovery has become a significant factor in litigation. Obviously, this has occurred because electronic records and electronic text documents are the primary forms of creating and storing information. Since this makes e-Discovery an important aspect of corporate life, how can Enterprise Architecture help to organize this complex issue?

First of all, this issue is technically similar to other issues that have occurred. Building data warehouses for business intelligence, integrating all financial information, tracking all corporate assets, business rules management, and managing the supply chain are some of the other major issues. Each of these issues has resulted in tentacles reaching out to all applications for information. These tentacles, like duct tape, have wrapped around the core applications and technologies to a point where corporate agility has almost been snuffed out.

E-Discovery is similar to these other issues in the approach to management as recommended by consultants. The recommendation is for a centralized "Records Management" group that works directly and regularly with IT. This means staffing another organization and extending the staff of IT. Oh, and let us not forget, this initiative will require senior management commitment.

Another approach, within the Enterprise Architecture, is the adoption of standards for defining integration points. The definition of these integration points would be under the authority of the existing line-of-business units. In this model, each line-of-business would work to maximize the reuse of existing integration points. They would shape the integration points from a business perspective. They would only call upon IT to provide new or improved integration points.

Each line-of-business would be responsible for guaranteeing that their retention policies are followed. They would provide the integration points to be used by the Corporate Legal Department's e-Discovery application. Legal would work with those having the greatest knowledge of the business, the management and staff of each line-of-business.

Just like the other issues listed, e-Discovery could be solved with a "quick and dirty" solution of more staff and duct tape. We can just dump the problem on IT again. Why not? IT understands all that technology stuff. Or, we could take a step back and realize we have done this before.

It is time to recognize that Enterprise Architecture can bring decentralization back. Each line-of-business can actually manage its own data. Not only can they do it, they can do it better at a much lower cost. E-Discovery is just one more reason for centralizing the models through Enterprise Architecture while decentralizing the control of IT.

Enterprise Architecture and Tough Economic Times

Rumor has it that Enterprise Architects live in an "Ivory Tower". During good times, they can join up with senior management and lay out plans to grow an organization and put in governance to make the best use of resources. This usually includes a "To Be" architecture that specifies some significant investment in infrastructure.

During tough times, when money and time is short, the Enterprise Architect's message does not seem relevant.

The senior management does not see any particular benefit for futuristic Enterprise Architects, the thought being that long-range strategic planning is less important when an organization is in a crisis of survival.

Should Enterprise Architects simply take the stand that the reason for the crisis was the lack of strategic planning in the first place? Enterprise Architects could simply say they told you so and write off any struggling organizations as poorly managed. Of course, this would be ridiculous. Organizations cannot predict the future. They do their best with strategic planning and focus on those things that will benefit the organization in both the short and long term.

So how can Enterprise Architects be relevant during tough times? Clearly, they must bring value to help move organizations out of their current crisis of survival. This means being an advocate for senior management and being skeptical of the value that the Corporate IT organization's ideas bring to the table.

Certainly, every Enterprise Architect agrees with being an advocate for senior management, but what about this skeptic thing? Shouldn't the Corporate IT organization be viewed as the provider of solutions? The answer is "No". Corporate IT organizations provide skilled resources and technologies to implement and operate the corporate solutions. But, the best solution providers are the corporate lines-of-business. It is each line-of-business that is trying to survive. They are the ones on the field playing the game. The Corporate IT organization is more like the cheerleaders.

What the Enterprise Architect can do is bring visualization of IT to each line-of-business. The Enterprise Architect can be a facilitator and a communicator that sets an environment for each line-of-business to innovate its own future.

Those that have the greatest potential to lose and gain during tough times, each line-of-business, should be supported by the Enterprise Architect. Enterprise Architects can be relevant by providing this support to help equip each line-of-business with the IT knowledge needed to win.

Before Knowledge Comes Understanding

Digging for Understanding

- *Thomas A. Tinsley*

Back in the 1990s, when the IT industry was trying to understand and properly apply Object-Oriented concepts, a book titled, *Design Patterns: Elements of Reusable Object-Oriented Software*[4] was published. This book opened up an entirely new way to look at OO. Many design pattern books have since followed with

4 Erich Gamma, Richard Helm, Ralph Johnson, John Vlissides, *Design Patterns: Elements of Reusable Object-Oriented Software* (Reading, MA: Addison Wesley, 1996).

specific attention to programming languages and infrastructure components.

As the story goes, the authors of this mind-changing book, dubbed as the "Gang of Four", were together at a conference and accidentally attended a session in the same hotel as their conference, but given for a different group. They attended a <u>building</u> architecture presentation. In the presentation the architect described the types of patterns that go into the design of a building. This includes things like locating all of the plumbing functions in the same area on a floor. They immediately recognized the parallels to building applications using objects.

As the Gang of Four looked outside of their discipline and drew parallels, I believe there are some great parallels between Archaeology and Enterprise Architects. Archaeologists often begin an excavation only to find that one city has been built upon another. How often does an Enterprise Architect find that the current internet layer of an organization has been built on top of a COBOL or a FORTRAN base? How many organizations are still running CICS or IMS? With all of the knowledge we have gained over the last 20 years about componentization, why is most processing still dependent upon procedural design?

There are answers to these questions, but first an Enterprise Architect must excavate and uncover the artifacts that make up a corporation's IT. This is the approach presented in my latest book, *Enterprise Architects: Masters of the Unseen City*[5]. Just for fun, you might find the personal interviews and the "photos" of the making of the book interesting. They can be found at: masters.selfserviceit.com.

Because of spatial technology, archaeologists can now organize uncovered artifacts and present a virtual view of lost cities. An Enterprise Architect can use this same technology to visualize IT. For each organization there is a specific city view. This view would contain the knowledge-base of their use of IT. Each line-of-business could then see what is for them today unseen.

This visualization could cause a major shift in how IT is used in an organization. I believe that this will result in an explosion of innovation.

---

5 Ibid., p.2

Current Thinking Obfuscating the Obvious

- *Thomas A. Tinsley*

Often we hear that solutions may be staring us in the face. Unfortunately, we are blinded by our inability to do what has been referred to as "Thinking outside the box". Great recommendations like "Step back and look at the entire picture" are just not part of the normal way of dealing with challenges.

Normally, a first assessment is to see how we can apply a solution to improve our current status-quo. This is happening with cloud computing. CIOs are looking at this concept as just another way to provision hardware and infrastructure. They seem to see it as simply an outgrowth of the virtualization concept. Technically, they may be correct, as CIOs usually are, but they have not stepped back.

In the book, *Seabiscuit, An American Legend*[6], Laura Hillenbrand describes how the automobile in the early 1900's was considered to be a nuisance. The automobile belched smoke, turned up dust, and would scare the horses. But, on April 18, 1906, things changed. A devastating earthquake hit San Francisco and fires broke out everywhere. The automobile proved its utility that day as an ambulance and as a transport that was not afraid of the fires. It was a beginning, but it still took years before automobiles became the primary means of transportation that we take for granted today.

Some believe that the recent economic disasters have awakened many to the benefits of cloud computing. We may have had our "1906 earthquake" in the 2008 market collapse. Most of the benefit is being attributed to the potential of reducing costs and supporting higher levels of innovation. It is seen as a new platform for

---

6 Laura Hillenbrand, *Seabiscuit* (New York: Ballantine Books, 2002).

business services. It is fostered as a new delivery model for Service-Oriented Architecture.

All of this seems to be right on target, but we still need to step back. Most organizations that let the Corporate IT group try SOA have shown little benefit. Applying this same approach across cloud services will probably result in the same disappointing outcomes.

Top-down visionaries are needed to organize and visually present the business services. Those that do this today practice the profession of Enterprise Architect. They have proven their value in successful SOA deployments. They put the business first and the technology infrastructure second. These are rare and valuable individuals that will naturally step back when looking at an organization and its use of technology. They do "think outside the box".

Enterprise Architects can bring the business value of cloud services from public, private, or hybrid clouds to an organization. Without an Enterprise Architect, the services would be pulled together creating a Tower of Babble. But, with an Enterprise Architect, cloud services would be organized into a clear understandable model. With this common language from the model, the business teams would be free to innovate across the entire enterprise.

He Should have Armed Himself

In the 1992 movie, "Unforgiven", directed by and starring Clint Eastwood, there was a typical Clint Eastwood scene. He enters a bar and gets the drop on all in the room, including the Sheriff. The Clint Eastwood character asks who the proprietor of the bar is. A man steps forward and the Clint Eastwood character shoots him dead. The Sheriff then says, "You shot an unarmed man!" The Clint Eastwood character then answers, "He should have armed himself."

The Sheriff had some notion that there were rules to be followed. Every fight should be a fair fight. It would be villainous to just shoot someone without giving them a chance. Translate this to the business world. Competitors should fight fair. If one is planning a great new product, it should let its competitors know so they would be prepared.

I worked at a bank several years back that developed a product that was primarily intended to go into grocery stores to guarantee checks. This would reduce the tremendous cost of bad checks being written. For a customer to use this self-service device, they only needed to sign up for an account and receive a plastic card with their identification information. It would work on any bank account.

If you are not aware, banks are very cordial to one another and most new products are not new at all. They are usually just a repackaging of existing services. Competition for the retail market is usually by the location of branches. Competition for the corporate market is usually by relationships and the size of loans that can be made.

When the bank introduced this check guarantee service, it was a great success. It was installed in grocery stores and other large retailers. Everyone was happy except the other banks in the city. They did not understand why they were not in on the planning. Why were they not able to get some of the business? They were given no chance to arm themselves. Why would they be shot this way? Senior managers of the competing banks tried to get the manager that launched this new service fired. The "good old boys" were not happy.

There are those that would like the business world to be fair with rules of competition as expected by the banks in this story. But, that is not the real world. Competition keeps our economy moving to new levels of benefit for all of us. It can also have great rewards for those that are first with a new idea.

Having a strong Enterprise Architecture is an important weapon to have when fighting competition. It can lay the foundation for an agile enterprise that is not only able to innovate and deliver greater value to their customers, but they will also be able to quickly respond when their competition introduces new innovations. So, do not be caught without arming yourself. There are those that do not play by the Sheriff's rules.

Are You a Bold Manager or a Gangster?

Culture is Hard to Change

- Thomas A. Tinsley

We have heard them all for years: "You can lead a horse to water, but you can't make him drink", "You can't teach an old dog new tricks", "You can't change the process, because we have always done it that way", and there are many more.

With all of this cumulative wisdom from the ages, why would anyone ever make *any* changes? The answer is simple: *there is probably money involved*. Companies get started because they have a new and, hopefully, better idea. New products are developed to reach new markets or to retain existing customers.

Corporate management must deal with the risk of change and at the same time the risk of not changing. During tough economic times, the easiest route is to not change. Management can trim resources and wait for the storm to pass. This is easier because change is minimized to staff reductions and expenditures that can wait. In these circumstances, management appears to be operating pragmatically. The management can survive while many of those that have worked hard for many years to attain success are cast aside to take the full burden of the economic downturn.

The "Godfather Movies" reflect the attitude of pragmatism that exists in organizations that do mass layoffs. The gangster solves problems by killing people and says that it is "just business". Corporate management can lay off thousands, denying them of an economic future. Most will eventually land a new position. Often they will need to pick up their families and move to another city. Many will drain their savings while looking for a new position. Some will become so depressed they are never able to work again. Some will lose their homes. Some will have their marriages end in divorce. Some will commit suicide. Some will go "postal" and kill innocent people. But, the management is being pragmatic about the company's survival. It is "just business".

Corporate management does have the choice to take on the high risk of change without downsizing. This requires a bold management team that looks upon the corporate staff as their greatest resource and will not let the current culture of the organization get in the way. This type of management looks to redefine the organization by realizing that it is not "just business". Bold managers recognize that corporations have a responsibility to their staff first and stockholders second.

IBM is an example of a company that has, when challenged, simply redefined itself and found a way to use its greatest resource, its people. Another company that has redefined itself is Amazon. When it was on the brink of financial disaster, it called in an Enterprise Architect to improve performance. What came out of this work far exceeded the original purpose. Amazon found that they could market their processes to other organizations as an entirely new business. IBM and Amazon have bold management that changed their company cultures. Amazon in particular was saved by a bold management team that recognized the importance of Enterprise Architecture.

So what type of manager are you? Are you bold? Are you more concerned about the corporate staff than you are your own hide? Or, are you a gangster levying pain upon others in the name of the business? If you are a gangster, I hope you did not get a bonus while destroying others' lives. I had rather think that you had turned to your Enterprise Architect and devised a bold plan to transition your company into a new successful culture.

You Do What?

Reflections on IT

- Thomas A. Tinsley

In my first book, *Deadlines and Duct Tape*[7], I told stories about my personal "duct tape" experiences as a manager in IT. It is amazing how much goes on under the cloak of invisibility worn by IT. This is a clear case where knowledge is power and IT has the technical knowledge and consequently holds the power.

_____

7 Ibid., p2

For those that can go behind the scene and actually see what is going on, they have to ask: "You did WHAT?" which is usually followed by some, "It's not MY fault", justification. Excuses are given such as the need to meet a deadline or management refused to purchase the software we needed. It is always someone else's fault.

Those like me that perform in the role of Enterprise Architect are advocates for the business. We see that this control of IT over the business must shift back to the business. Now keep in mind, Enterprise Architects have a clear understanding of the complexity of technology. We know that this complexity must be controlled by senior technical staff. So, the control that needs to shift is not the technical complexity, but rather the control of the business application of the technologies.

In my second book, *Enterprise Architects: Masters of the Unseen City*[8], I refer to those that manage and maintain the technical complexity of technology as the "Lords of the Underworld". I did this to emphasize their importance. They have the difficult task of guaranteeing the performance of their technology services. Talking to these guys, for any business manager, would be like

---

8 Ibid., p.2

going into the Underworld where people speak strange languages. In the Underworld, orders are given by the Lords and they must be followed to the letter or else chaos would reign.

The business should establish performance goals for the Lords of the Underworld, but not interfere in how they accomplish their goals. If they are not meeting their goals, then get someone else. Today, management has more options to select from. Options such as cloud computing are available to carry the heavy burden of high-performance infrastructure.

Just like in a city, we want our utilities underground. In a city, we can access the water, sewer, electric, and communication services at the surface with well-defined outlets. In Information Technology, we should be able to tap in without needing to understand the underlying technologies. Having this access gives the business management access to the business information and processes.

So how can this be accomplished? Is there a magic wand? Is there a software package available? The answer is Enterprise Architecture. It is not magic and it is not a package. It is basic hard work to establish the service layer at the city level. To do this will require Enterprise Architects.

So do not be scared. Do not venture into the Underworld. Call upon an Enterprise Architect to change the unseen city to a city that can be seen. Learn how by reading my book, *Enterprise Architects: Masters of the Unseen City*[9].

---

9   Ibid., p.2

Can You Kill Jason?

- Thomas A. Tinsley

Jason cannot be killed. He keeps on coming back for more money. He has done quite well doing the "Halloween" movies and has little reason to ever stop. We don't even know who he is since he always wears a hockey mask. Somehow, this entire description is very similar to Corporate IT. No matter who wears the mask, they just keep on coming back for more money.

Just like we are getting tired of Jason in the movies, we are all looking for something better from Corporate IT. It is time for a change. We need some new approaches.

We need to feel that thrill again. We are tired of the mask. We are tired of the excessive cost and delays of Corporate IT.

What we need is a hero. We need someone that can break down the barriers and let us see behind the mask. We have so many great changes already taking place. We have the ability to do business process management and data mashups. We can use cloud computing infrastructure and applications. We can communicate in ways we are only beginning to understand with our cell phones and our internet browsers. With all of this change, we need a hero to come on the scene and let us see how everything can actually fit together to the benefit of the business.

If you have followed my blog or read my latest book, you know who the hero is. The Enterprise Architects are the heroes. They are the mild-mannered reporters that have super-human understanding of the complexity of IT. And, even though they can speak fluently with the Lords of the Underworld in Corporate IT, they can also provide business management with the visibility needed to see behind the mask.

Enterprise Architects can put the flood lights on Corporate IT. This is like exposing a vampire to the sunlight. The vampire looses power and dies. The same awaits Corporate IT. Once exposed, only those in the Underworld will survive. Those on the surface that wear a mask and continually ask for more and more will not survive. They will be overcome by the light that the Enterprise Architect brings to the business managers.

So, Jason may not be able to be killed. But, the powerful Corporate IT we know today will find its demise. The hero, the Enterprise Architect, will accomplish this by bringing visualization of IT to the business. He is fully armed to take on this challenge with the modeling views that have been developed by the masters of IT over the last few decades. For details, order your copy of my book, *Enterprise Architects: Masters of the Unseen City*[10].

---

10 Ibid., p.2

Aging Software is Good

- Thomas A. Tinsley

Corporate IT has some great terms like "legacy systems" to describe applications designed and developed in the "old days" of technology. If we look upon application systems like factory equipment, this idea of "old" is a strong consideration for "modernization". How could anyone running a software application written in an older technology not want to bring it up to a modern technology?

Well, is it reasonable to compare application software with factory equipment? Factory equipment wears out and parts need to be replaced. Software does not show any wear and never needs parts replaced. Obviously, this is why it is called software rather than hardware. So, to answer the question, application software never actually wears out.

But, what about maintenance and support? As newer development languages come out, isn't it difficult to get support for the older languages? Although it may be more difficult to get support, it can almost always be found somewhere. But, what about the cost? Doesn't the cost of maintenance go up for older development languages? Actually, the more expensive development is always with the new languages. With new languages there is usually a smaller pool of available resources.

Maybe the concept of modernization has nothing to do with the way the software was developed. Maybe the software simply does not deliver the functionality that is needed by the business. Well, this does not make any sense at all. The business operates every day just fine with the old software. If it did not provide the needed functionality, the business would be out of business.

Alright, it does not wear out, maintenance can be provided, and it meets the business needs. Why modernize? Business management is told by Corporate IT that the older applications must be modernized to bring about agility in a changing business environment. They say there must be a movement away from silo applications where information is not shared and processes cannot be reused. These are lofty platitudes that imply a complete rewrite of the current applications.

Often, Corporate IT uses these lofty goals as a means of justifying major enhancements in the IT infrastructure. Enhancements may include things like message systems, service-oriented architecture control systems, and new development environments. Besides the cost of this new infrastructure, there is the cost associated with the IT staff and the users learning how to effectively use the new environment. And, there is, of course, the cost of errors due to conditions not considered in the development of the new software.

Enterprise Architects follow the approach that silo applications are like fine wine. They get better with age. The software has been time-tested. Business conditions that the original developers overlooked have long since been corrected. These applications are good, they work, and they are a major asset of the business. They may even be paid for!

The Enterprise Architect realizes that all change must be driven by business needs. For example, if the company's competition is offering faster response to service requests due to better applications, then change may be required to stay competitive. If the Enterprise Architect has organized the current IT artifacts as described in *Enterprise Architects: Masters of the Unseen City*[11], then it will be visually obvious where changes are needed. Usually, only parts of an application will need to be changed. These changes would expose the needed integration points.

Taking this incremental approach will minimize the risk of change, the cost of change, and the time required to implement the change. Over time, the entire application may get replaced component by component. There may even be a time when the cost of maintaining the older components is not cost-justified. At that time, the remaining components could be scheduled for upgrading.

Enterprise Architects do not use the terms "modernization" and "legacy". They focus on business needs and the minimization of change to bring true business value.

---

11 Ibid., p.2

Chicago-Style IT

- Thomas A. Tinsley

When a corporation needs to cut costs, it usually takes a top-down approach. The top five major budget areas will be considered. The first and usually the largest for any corporation is the payroll. Jobs can be eliminated and the company can continue to operate. The IT budget will often show up in the top five of the list as well. Since the corporation does not fully understand what makes up the IT budget, they turn the cutting question over to the CIO.

Corporate management realizes that Information Technology is important to the corporation and does not demand cuts without some justification. They look at third-party reports that give them a good idea of what the IT budget should be. They see what other comparable organizations are doing and expect their IT to do the same.

When cuts are demanded, the CIO is forced to not only make staff cuts, but other cuts as well. This is a sort of double whammy for being such a large part of the corporate expenditures. This is a difficult challenge since it must be met by keeping everything that is currently in operation in a running state.

CIOs are forced to stop IT-specific expenditures immediately. Decisions might include stopping hardware upgrades, stopping the purchase of new software, eliminate attending conferences, and dropping the renewal of publications. There would probably be efforts to redefine contracts to get a better deal. Even the coffee pot may go away!

These knee-jerk decisions are only a reflection of poor IT management trying to survive. Had the IT management been doing the job well, they would have a budget below the industry norm and they would probably not be asked to make additional cuts.

The corporate management is right to expect their IT budget to be close to the norm. But, they are also responsible for making sure this is taking place during good times as well as bad. They need to know that their IT organization is performing equal to or better than comparable organizations. If they are performing much better than comparable organizations then IT will probably not be asked to make additional cuts.

Good IT management recognizes the importance of Enterprise Architects. They know that Enterprise Architects pursue holistic approaches that result in lower costs. They know that Enterprise Architects are driven by business needs and are drivers of fun technologies. They are supportive of the visualization that the Enterprise Architects bring to the business as described in *Enterprise Architects: Masters of the Unseen City*[12]. They know that the more the corporate management understands about the value of IT, the less likely the chance that IT will be asked to cut their budget during difficult times.

---

12 Ibid., p.2

If It Ain't Broke...

The Unseen Can Hurt You

New CIO	Enterprise Architect
Just turn off the mainframe!	You'll get a quick response!
We'll see who uses that old technology!	That will stop Payroll!

- *Thomas A. Tinsley*

In 1991 Robert J. Kriegel and Louis Patler wrote the book, *If it Ain't Broke ... BREAK IT!*[13] In this book the authors challenged managers to not accept doing things the way they have always been done. He built on the idea that anything can be improved. In his book there are memorable chapters like, "Sacred Cows Make the Best Burgers".

---

13 Robert J. Kriegel and Louis Patler, *If it Ain't Broke ... BREAK IT!* (New York, NY: Warner Books, Inc., 1992).

This attitude of change does not seem to have much of a place in the world of Information Technology. In this world there is more of an effort to figure out how to embrace the enormous amount of change that continues to take place. This is a world of great excitement as advancements in computer speed, storage capacity, and network capabilities seem to run ahead of our ability to innovate applications.

Those entering into this world for the first time as IT Professionals are often wrapped up in one or more of the major areas of advancement. They can visualize opportunities and how they can individually bring their vision to reality. They are eager to jump in and take advantage of the latest technologies and methodologies.

Unfortunately, when an individual joins a large organization where Information Technology is only used to support their primary business the reality they find is not very exciting. Most organizations are still running applications developed ten, twenty, or even thirty years ago. At the speed of change in Information Technology, these applications are considered to be ancient. They are written in languages like COBOL, Fortran, and PL/1. These languages were used before man landed on the moon.

These ancient applications written in ancient tongues are usually the backbone of an organization. They do the heavy lifting that gets the orders fulfilled, the financial transactions posted, the resources tracked, and so forth. They are the true reality of Information Technology in most large organizations.

Anyone choosing to break one of these ancient applications would be risking the survival of the business. They would be risking their job. Besides, it works. Why change just for the sake of change?

Baby boomers that entered the world of Information Technology back in the ancient times are still part of the workforce and are maintaining the old core systems. They have the deep experience needed to keep everything running. They can speak with authority on the topics of CICS, IMS, MVS, UNIX, and MQ Series. Those joining organizations using these ancient technologies must simply adapt. They must change their visualization of the future.

For some joining an organization, they may be part of the new web-enabled applications. These applications are used as delivery tools for the ancient applications. They provide the customer interface on the web, in the stores, and within the organization. Often, they replicate data and processes from the ancient applications. They do this because reuse cannot cross over the technology boundaries.

Clearly, there must be an enterprise view of the business. There must be a view that will <u>not</u> fracture the excitement of the new individuals entering into Information Technology. There must be a view that supports the validity of the ancient applications or a plan to upgrade them. There must be a well-defined Enterprise Architecture developed by Enterprise Architects in conjunction with the business and the Corporate IT department.

There must be visualization of IT for all. There must be self-service IT for all.

We Have Our Backs to the Wall

Perception Beats Reality

- *Thomas A. Tinsley*

I have not yet met a Corporate IT department that did not have a backlog. I have never met a Corporate IT department that is not working against a tight schedule to deliver new functionality. But, every Corporate IT department I have met has over a third of its staff wasting their time on frivolous projects or sitting idle just waiting for something to do.

First, let's look at production in IT. The production line is fully automated. Any manual efforts are by choice. In any well-run shop, the staff is only there to monitor the process. The days of mounting tapes and loading disk drives are long past. Even the printing operations are moving to web delivery. So who is sitting idle? The problem handlers are sitting idle. They are like the "Maytag Repair Man". They have nothing to do until something actually breaks.

So what do the repair guys do all day? They usually work together on what they call improvement projects. These projects are usually born out of a past failure that could have been prevented had this new improvement been installed. Of course, they take a broader look and take into account even other conditions that might happen as well. This keeps them busy and gives them something to report on during status update meetings.

The other part of Corporate IT, Development and Support, is always busy. This staff is driven by project management. There are senior project managers that map out plans and resource requirements. They can show the critical path to meeting the required implementation deadline.

Whether the plan is developed using the "Waterfall" method or the "Agile" method, there is always a need for individuals with varied skills. Consequently, there is always slack time in the plan. This is time when one group or individual must wait on another before they can begin. For example, quality testers have little to do before there is something to test. Technical writers have little to do until there is something to write about. Developers cannot write process code until there are databases.

Corporate IT has tried to address this problem with multiple organizational approaches. One approach is to organize departments around technical skills. With a large volume of projects, this organization can minimize idle time although it seems to delay projects. As an example, most organizations have centralized their database development and maintenance. They even go so far as to have separate groups for each vendor's database.

In another approach, team members can be cross-trained so they can work multiple tasks within a project. This does reduce idle time, but often requires more time to accomplish tasks with less quality when compared to the work done by those that are highly skilled in a technology.

The "Agile" project methodology is one of the best for keeping everyone on a project busy. With the daily standup meetings with everyone involved, management can attend and get the sense that everyone is focused on the target. This method should prevent work being done as the result of miscommunications. But, it does not solve the problem of idle time.

The answer to production is easy. Move to cloud computing. The senior technology professionals needed to solve problems and maintain the infrastructure would be in the cloud. These individuals will serve many customers and probably find little idle time. Those in the business organization that are running and monitoring the production would have little idle time.

Solving the "development of new applications" challenge is simple, but not so easy. Start with a full visualization of the current use of Information Technology. This can be done by your Enterprise Architects working with the lines-of-business and with Corporate IT. The visualization should show all of the integration points and integration point references of the existing applications. The integration points and their references should be catalogued according to the business's specific process and data models. This can be done in a few weeks depending upon the size of the organization and the number of applications.

At this point, everyone will have a visual representation of their use of Information Technology. Then, based upon the priorities of changes needed and with the help of the Enterprise Architect, identify where integration points can be exposed for use or where new integration points need to be created. For those integration points, consider allowing the line-of-business to implement appropriate consumption technology. These technologies include business process management, mashups, and portals.

For those integration points that do not exist due to new business requirements, consider SaaS in the cloud. If no SaaS services are available, consider putting out a Request for Proposal (RFP) to have them constructed by someone other than your Corporate IT. These services can be added to your private cloud.

These approaches seem far out, yet consider what is taking place. The old days of centralized Corporate IT are being challenged by more economical resource usage and a need to allow each line-of-business to innovate their own future. This approach is described in the book, *Enterprise Architects: Masters of the Unseen City*[14].

By applying the principles of Enterprise Architecture, you can cut the idle time, cut the backlog, and manage tight schedules from a business perspective. This will add up to very significant savings.

---

14 Ibid., p.2

About the Author

Tom Tinsley is an Enterprise Architect who has a personal goal to promote the value of his profession and its promise through a series of books, blogs, articles and lectures. He has worked in IT, including senior management positions for banks, state government and other companies and organizations, for many years.

After years of managing Information Technology as a Vice President in Banking and as a Director in State Government, Tom turned to strategy and mentoring as an Enterprise Architect. He has led Enterprise Architecture in the retail industry and the media industry to achieve a common vision for the use of computing technology to meet business goals.

His personal passion has been to bridge the gap between Business Management and Information Technology. Tom has published many internal documents and given multiple speeches and presentations to further the awareness of new opportunities and the application of best practices. He recognizes the need for business management to play a greater role in the actions of Information Technology. He sees this as a win-win where Business Management can focus on servicing their customers and Information

Technology can focus on providing reliable, high-performance, automated services.

Other Books by Thomas A. Tinsley

Enterprise Architects: Masters of the Unseen City describes how Enterprise Architects can facilitate changes to allow innovative business managers to

visualize their Corporate IT, leading to higher revenue, lower costs, and reduced delivery time.

Follow Hope the intern and the Enterprise Architect as they excavate IT. Like archaeologists, they plan their dig, select their tools, uncover models, and discover IT artifacts. Their adventure takes them into the territory of the Lords of the Underworld. They show how to protect their dig and bring all the models together into a holistic model as a virtual city, providing the Corporate Office full visual access to their use of IT.

They discover that cloud computing, social networking, and virtual reality are mixing and exploding into an unprecedented level of innovation.

masters.SelfServiceIT.com.

Deadlines and Duct Tape: A Manifesto for the Business Managers to Understand and Direct IT describes the communications gap between the business and Information Technology (IT). The book presents a Manifesto for Business Managers to understand and direct IT. If you are a business manager that is in the dark on how IT performs critical functions and you feel that IT is running your business, then this book is for you. If you are an IT manager that feels like life is nothing but a series of deadlines, then this book is for you.

mkpress.com

www.ingramcontent.com/pod-product-compliance
Lightning Source LLC
Chambersburg PA
CBHW061029050326
40689CB00012B/2740